MEL BAY PRESENTS

VIHUELA
Chord Dictionary
Presented in English and Spanish

by José Guadalupe Alfaro

The Mexican vihuela is a descendant of the Renaissance instrument of the same name that was a favorite of the Spanish court during the fifteenth and sixteenth centuries. It was introduced into Mexico in 1519 by a Spanish musician by the last name of Ortiz who accompanied conquistador Hernán Cortés.* Mexican natives soon learned to build this instrument, making their own modifications both to its construction and manner of playing. Although the vihuela died out in Spain, it became a popular folk instrument in Mexico. The Mexican vihuela is an indispensable ingredient of the contemporary mariachi group.

*Alejo Carpentier et al. Music in Cuba. (Minneapolis: University of Minnesota Press, 2001), 68.

La vihuela mexicana desciende del instrumento renacentista del mismo nombre, favorito de la corte española durante los siglos XV y XVI. Fue introducida a México en 1519 por un músico español de apellido Ortiz que acompañaba al conquistador Hernán Cortés. Los mexicanos pronto dominaron su confección, haciendo sus propias modificaciones en su construcción tanto en la manera de tocarla. En España la vihuela desapareció, mientras que en México se arraigó como instrumento folclórico. La vihuela mexicana es imprescindible para el conjunto de mariachi contemporáneo.*

*Alejo Carpentier. La música en Cuba. (La Habana: Editorial Letras Cubanas, 1979), 20.

I wish to express my gratitude, admiration, and respect to Jonathan Clark for his invaluable support, effort, and collaboration in making this book a reality.

Quiero expresar mi agradecimiento, admiración y respeto al Lic. Jonathan Clark por su invaluable apoyo, esfuerzo y colaboración para la realización de este libro".

Cover photo courtesy of Candelas Guitars
Traditional Standard Vihuela by Tomás Delgado, Candelas Guitars
For more info visit: www.candelas.com

1 2 3 4 5 6 7 8 9 0

Table of Contents

Tabla de Contenido

Chord symbols

Each note of the musical scale is represented by a capital letter of the alphabet. These same letters are used for naming chords.

A = la

B = si

C = do

D = re

E = mi

F = fa

G = sol

The following letters, symbols, and abbreviations are used in this book:

m (lower case) = minor

♭ = flat

♯ = sharp

+ = augmented

º (small circle) = diminished

maj = Major seven

The following are examples of chord symbols:

A = A major	A♯m = A-sharp minor
Am = A minor	A+ = A augmented
A♭ = A-flat major	Aº = A diminished
A♭m = A-flat minor	A7 = A seven
A♯ = A-sharp major	Amaj7 = A major seven

Chords separated by (↔) are enharmonic: two chords sharing the same notes and fingerings, but named differently. Example: A-sharp and B-flat: A♯ ↔ B♭.

Other enharmonic equivalents: C♯ ↔ D♭, D♯ ↔ E♭, F♯ ↔ G♭, G♯ ↔ A♭.

Cifrado de los acordes

A cada nota de la escala musical le corresponde una letra mayúscula. Estas mismas letras se usan para cifrar los acordes.

A = la

B = si

C = do

D = re

E = mi

F = fa

G = sol

En este libro, se usan las siguientes letras, signos y abreviaturas:

m (minúscula) = menor

♭ = bemol

♯ = sostenido

+ = aumentado

º (círculo pequeño) = disminuido

maj = séptima mayor

Algunos ejemplos del cifrado de acordes:

A = la mayor	A♯m = la sostenido menor
Am = la menor	A+ = la aumentado
A♭ = la bemol mayor	Aº = la disminuido
A♭m = la bemol menor	A7 = la siete
A♯ = la sostenido mayor	Amaj7 = la séptima mayor

Los acordes que aparecen separados por una flecha de doble cabeza (↔) son enarmónicos. Ejemplo: La sostenido y Si bemol A♯ ↔ B♭.

Otras equivalencias enarmónicas: C♯ ↔ D♭, D♯ ↔ E♭, F♯ ↔ G♭, G♯ ↔ A♭.

The following examples explain the symbols used in the chord diagrams.
Los siguientes ejemplos explican los símbolos usados en los diagramas para los acordes.

The vertical lines represent the strings.
Las líneas verticales representan las cuerdas.

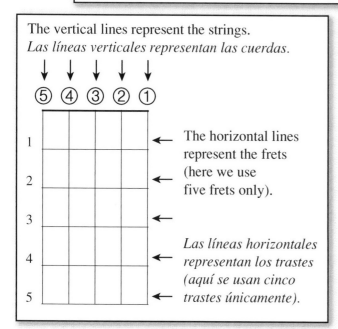

The horizontal lines represent the frets (here we use five frets only).

Las líneas horizontales representan los trastes (aquí se usan cinco trastes únicamente).

The white numbers inside the black circle represent the fingers on the left hand ("P" stands for *pulgar* or thumb).

index finger	**1**	*dedo índice*
middle finger	**2**	*dedo medio*
ring finger	**3**	*dedo anular*
little finger	**4**	*dedo meñique*
thumb	**P**	*dedo pulgar*

A cada dedo de la mano izquierda le corresponde un número (a excepción del dedo pulgar que se indica con la letra "P").

Open string names
Nombre de las cuerdas al aire

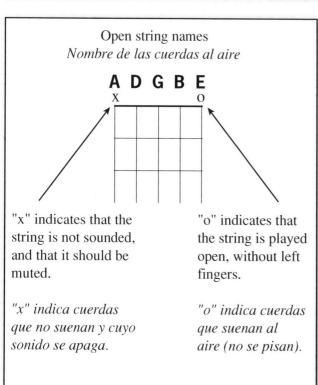

"x" indicates that the string is not sounded, and that it should be muted.

"x" indica cuerdas que no suenan y cuyo sonido se apaga.

"o" indicates that the string is played open, without left fingers.

"o" indica cuerdas que suenan al aire (no se pisan).

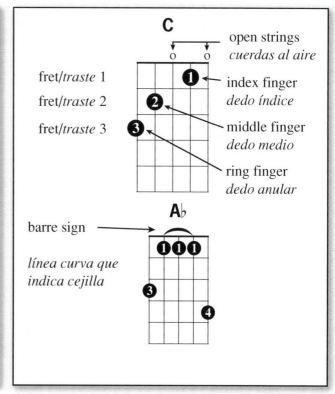

5

major
mayor

C	C♯ ↔ D♭	D
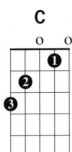	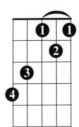	

D♯ ↔ E♭	E	F
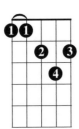	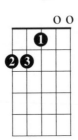	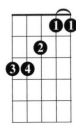

F♯ ↔ G♭	G	G♯ ↔ A♭
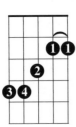	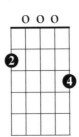	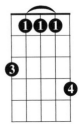

A	A♯ ↔ B♭	B
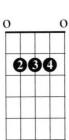	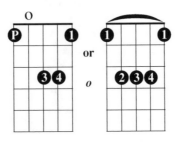	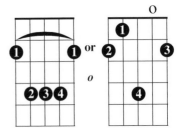

Note: Major chords are indicated simply by the letter name of their root, with no suffix or extension.
Nota: Los acordes mayores se indican únicamente con la letra de su nota fundamental, sin sufijo o extensión.

♭5
major flat five
mayor con quinta bemol

C^(♭5)

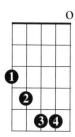

C^{#(♭5)} ↔ D^{♭(♭5)}

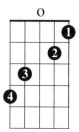

D^(♭5)

D^{#(♭5)} ↔ E^{♭(♭5)}

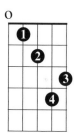

E^(♭5)

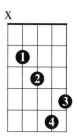

F^(♭5)

F^{#(♭5)} ↔ G^{♭(♭5)}

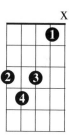

G^(♭5)

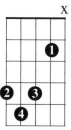

G^{#(♭5)} ↔ A^{♭(♭5)}

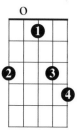

A^(♭5)

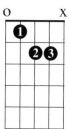

A^{#(♭5)} ↔ B^{♭(♭5)}

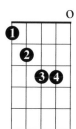

B^(♭5)

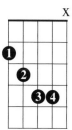

6
major sixth
mayor seis

C^6

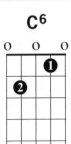

C$^{\#}$6 ↔ D$^{\flat}$6

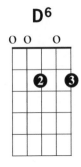

D^6

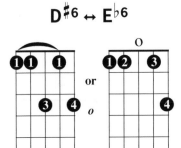

D$^{\#}$6 ↔ E$^{\flat}$6

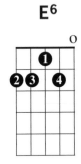

E^6

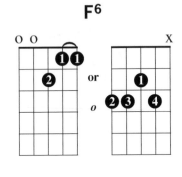

F^6

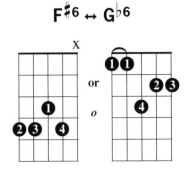

F$^{\#}$6 ↔ G$^{\flat}$6

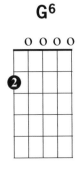

G^6

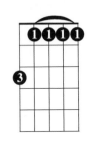

G$^{\#}$6 ↔ A$^{\flat}$6

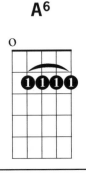

A^6

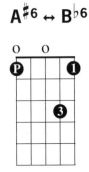

A$^{\#}$6 ↔ B$^{\flat}$6

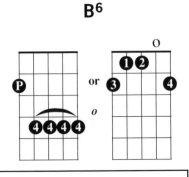

B^6

Note that the chords on this page have enharmonic equivalents in the minor seventh chords on page 17.
Nota que los acordes de esta página tienen equivalencias enarmónicas con los de séptima menor Triada la página 17.

6/9
six-nine
seis nueve

C⁶/⁹

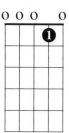

C♯⁶/⁹ ↔ D♭⁶/⁹

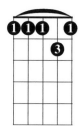

D⁶/⁹

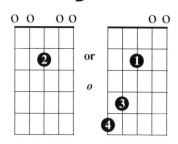

D♯⁶/⁹ ↔ E♭⁶/⁹

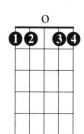

E⁶/⁹

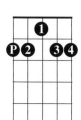

F⁶/⁹

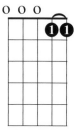

F♯⁶/⁹ ↔ G♭⁶/⁹

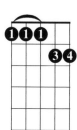

G⁶/⁹

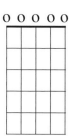

G♯⁶/⁹ ↔ A♭⁶/⁹

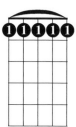

A⁶/⁹

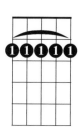

A♯⁶/⁹ ↔ B♭⁶/⁹

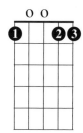

B⁶/⁹

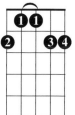

(add 9)
major add nine
mayor con novena adherida

C$^{(add\ 9)}$

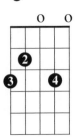

C$\sharp^{(add\ 9)}$ ↔ D$\flat^{(add\ 9)}$

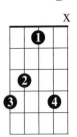

D$^{(add\ 9)}$

D$\sharp^{(add\ 9)}$ ↔ E$\flat^{(add\ 9)}$

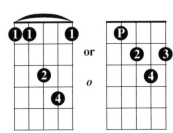

E$^{(add\ 9)}$

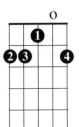

F$^{(add\ 9)}$

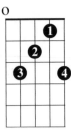

F$\sharp^{(add\ 9)}$ ↔ G$\flat^{(add\ 9)}$

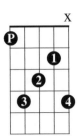

G$^{(add\ 9)}$

G$\sharp^{(add\ 9)}$ ↔ A$\flat^{(add\ 9)}$

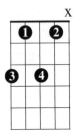

A$^{(add\ 9)}$

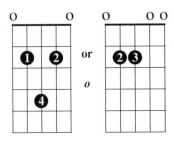

A$\sharp^{(add\ 9)}$ ↔ B$\flat^{(add\ 9)}$

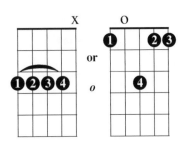

B$^{(add\ 9)}$

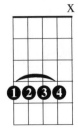

maj⁷
major seven
séptima mayor

C$_{maj}$⁷

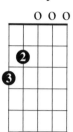

C#$_{maj}$⁷ ↔ D♭$_{maj}$⁷

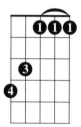

D$_{maj}$⁷

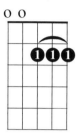

D#$_{maj}$⁷ ↔ E♭$_{maj}$⁷

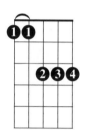

E$_{maj}$⁷

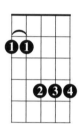

F$_{maj}$⁷

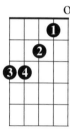

F#$_{maj}$⁷ ↔ G♭$_{maj}$⁷

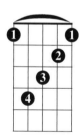

G$_{maj}$⁷

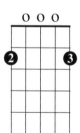

G#$_{maj}$⁷ ↔ A♭$_{maj}$⁷

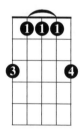

A$_{maj}$⁷

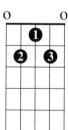

A#$_{maj}$⁷ ↔ B♭$_{maj}$⁷

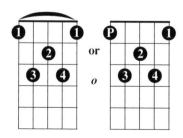

B$_{maj}$⁷

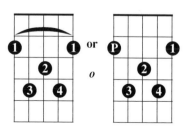

maj⁷⁽♭⁵⁾
major seven flat five
séptima mayor con quinta bemol

Cmaj⁷⁽♭⁵⁾

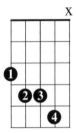

C♯maj⁷⁽♭⁵⁾ ↔ D♭maj⁷⁽♭⁵⁾

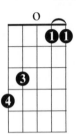

Dmaj⁷⁽♭⁵⁾

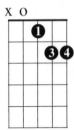

D♯maj⁷⁽♭⁵⁾ ↔ E♭maj⁷⁽♭⁵⁾

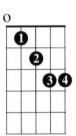

Emaj⁷⁽♭⁵⁾

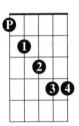

Fmaj⁷⁽♭⁵⁾

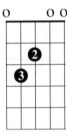

F♯maj⁷⁽♭⁵⁾ ↔ G♭maj⁷⁽♭⁵⁾

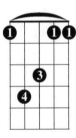

Gmaj⁷⁽♭⁵⁾

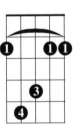

G♯maj⁷⁽♭⁵⁾ ↔ A♭maj⁷⁽♭⁵⁾

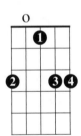

Amaj⁷⁽♭⁵⁾

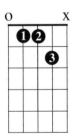

A♯maj⁷⁽♭⁵⁾ ↔ B♭maj⁷⁽♭⁵⁾

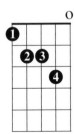

Bmaj⁷⁽♭⁵⁾

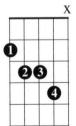

maj⁹
major nine
mayor con novena

C maj⁹
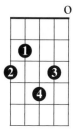

C♯maj⁹ ↔ D♭maj⁹
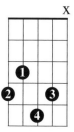

D maj⁹

D♯maj⁹ ↔ E♭maj⁹
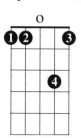

E maj⁹
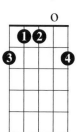

F maj⁹

F♯maj⁹ ↔ G♭maj⁹
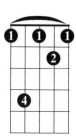

G maj⁹
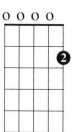

G♯maj⁹ ↔ A♭maj⁹
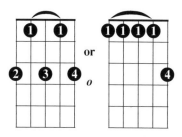

A maj⁹
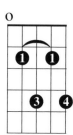

A♯maj⁹ ↔ D♭maj⁹
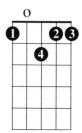

B maj⁹
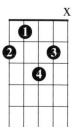

m
minor
menor

Cm
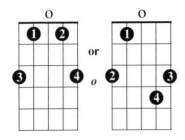

C#m ↔ D♭m
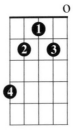

Dm

D#m ↔ E♭m
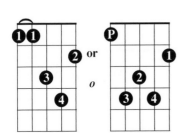

Em
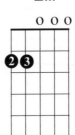

Fm
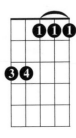

F#m ↔ G♭m
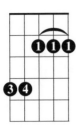

Gm
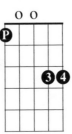

G#m ↔ A♭m
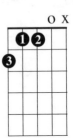

Am
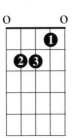

A#m ↔ B♭m
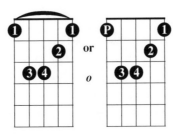

Bm
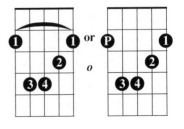

m⁶
minor six
menor seis

Cm⁶

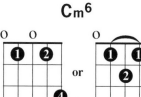

C♯m⁶ ↔ D♭m⁶

Dm⁶

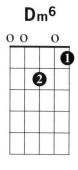

D♯m⁶ ↔ E♭m⁶

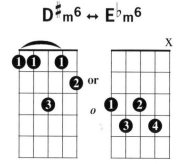

Em⁶

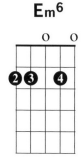

Fm⁶

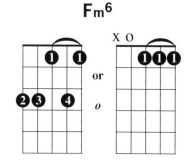

F♯m⁶ ↔ G♭m⁶

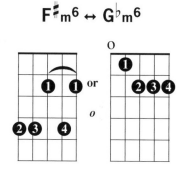

Gm⁶

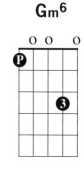

G♯m⁶ ↔ A♭m⁶

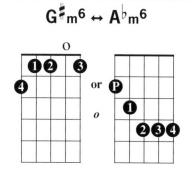

Am⁶

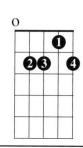

A♯m⁶ ↔ B♭m⁶

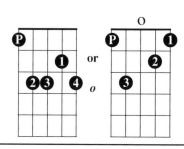

Bm⁶

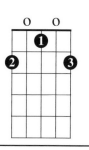

Note that the chords on this page have enharmonic equivalents in the minor seven flat five chords on page 19.
Nota que los acordes de esta página tienen equivalencias enarmónicas con los de séptima menor quinta bemol
de la página 19.

m6/9
minor six nine
menor seis nueve

Cm6/9

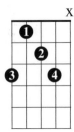

C#m6/9 ↔ D♭m6/9

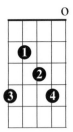

Dm6/9

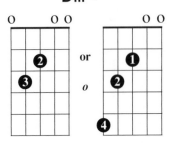

D#m6/9 ↔ E♭m6/9

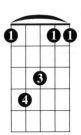

Em6/9

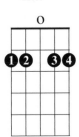

Fm6/9

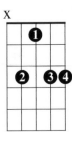

F#m6/9 ↔ G♭m6/9

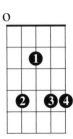

Gm6/9

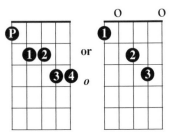

G#m6/9 ↔ A♭m6/9

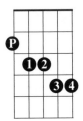

Am6/9

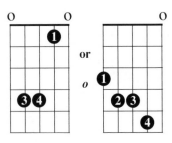

A#m6/9 ↔ B♭m6/9

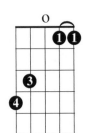

Bm6/9

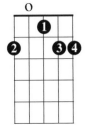

m⁷
minor seven
menor siete

Cm⁷
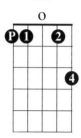

C♯m⁷ ↔ D♭m⁷
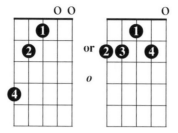

Dm⁷
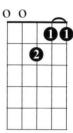

D♯m⁷ ↔ E♭m⁷
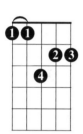

Em⁷
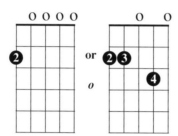

Fm⁷
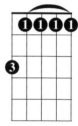

F♯m⁷ ↔ G♭m⁷
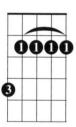

Gm⁷
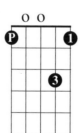

G♯m⁷ ↔ A♭m⁷
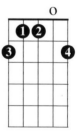

Am⁷
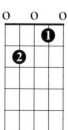

A♯m⁷ ↔ B♭m⁷
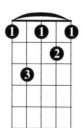

Bm⁷
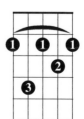

m(maj7)
minor with major seventh
menor con séptima mayor

Cm(maj7)

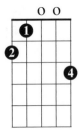

C#m(maj7) ↔ D♭m(maj7)

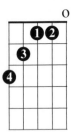

Dm(maj7)

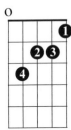

D#m(maj7) ↔ E♭m(maj7)

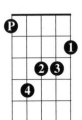

Em(maj7)

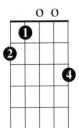

Fm(maj7)

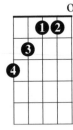

F#m(maj7) ↔ G♭m(maj7)

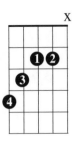

Gm(maj7)

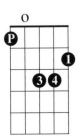

G#m(maj7) ↔ A♭m(maj7)

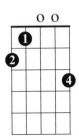

Am(maj7)

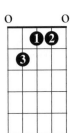

A#m(maj7) ↔ B♭m(maj7)

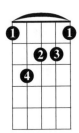

Bm(maj7)

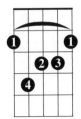

m⁷⁽♭⁵⁾
minor seven flat five
menor siete con quinta bemol

Cm⁷⁽♭⁵⁾

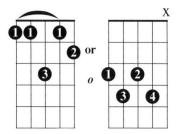

C♯m⁷⁽♭⁵⁾ ↔ D♭m⁷⁽♭⁵⁾

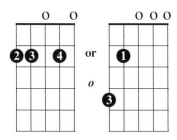

Dm⁷⁽♭⁵⁾

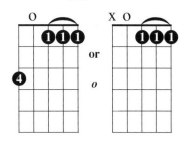

D♯m⁷⁽♭⁵⁾ ↔ E♭m⁷⁽♭⁵⁾

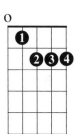

Em⁷⁽♭⁵⁾

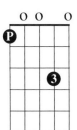

Fm⁷⁽♭⁵⁾

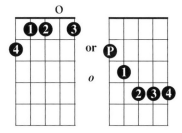

F♯m⁷⁽♭⁵⁾ ↔ G♭m⁷⁽♭⁵⁾

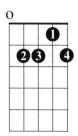

Gm⁷⁽♭⁵⁾

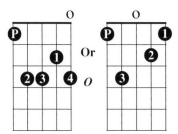

G♯m⁷⁽♭⁵⁾ ↔ A♭m⁷⁽♭⁵⁾

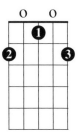

Am⁷⁽♭⁵⁾

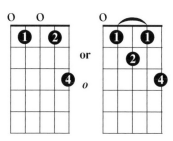

A♯m⁷⁽♭⁵⁾ ↔ B♭m⁷⁽♭⁵⁾

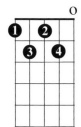

Bm⁷⁽♭⁵⁾

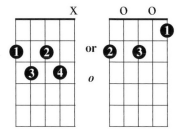

m⁹
minor nine
menor nueve

Cm⁹

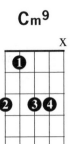

C♯m⁹ ↔ D♭m⁹

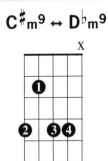

Dm⁹

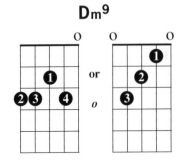

D♯m⁹ ↔ E♭m⁹

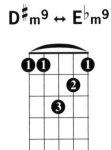

Em⁹

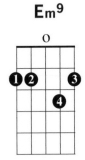

Fm⁹

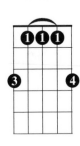

F♯m⁹ ↔ G♭m⁹

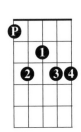

Gm⁹

G♯m⁹ ↔ A♭m⁹

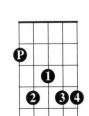

Am⁹

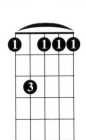

A♯m⁹ ↔ B♭m⁹

Bm⁹

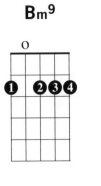

m^{11}
minor eleven
menor once

Cm^{11}
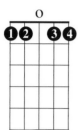

C$^\sharp$m^{11} ↔ D$^\flat$m^{11}
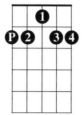

Dm^{11}
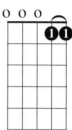

D$^\sharp$m^{11} ↔ E$^\flat$m^{11}
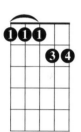

Em^{11}
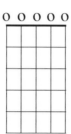

Fm^{11}
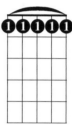

F$^\sharp$m^{11} ↔ G$^\flat$m^{11}
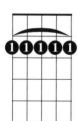

Gm^{11}
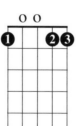

G$^\sharp$m^{11} ↔ A$^\flat$m^{11}
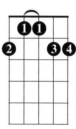

Am^{11}
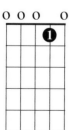

A$^\sharp$m^{11} ↔ B$^\flat$m^{11}
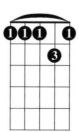

Bm^{11}
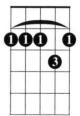

7
seven
siete

C⁷

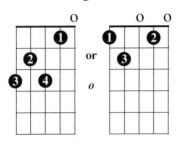

C♯⁷ ↔ D♭⁷

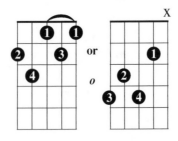

D⁷

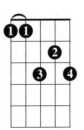

D♯⁷ ↔ E♭⁷

E⁷

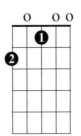

F⁷

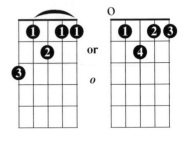

F♯⁷ ↔ G♭⁷

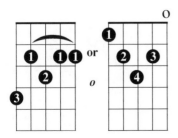

G⁷

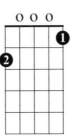

G♯⁷ ↔ A♭⁷

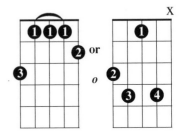

A⁷

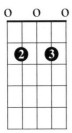

A♯⁷ ↔ B♭⁷

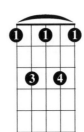

B⁷

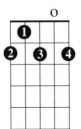

7(♭5)
seven flat five
siete con quinta bemol

C⁷⁽♭5⁾

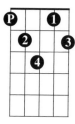

C#⁷⁽♭5⁾ ↔ D♭⁷⁽♭5⁾

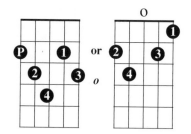

D⁷⁽♭5⁾

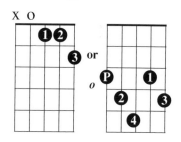

D#⁷⁽♭5⁾ ↔ E♭⁷⁽♭5⁾

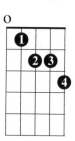

E⁷⁽♭5⁾

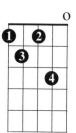

F⁷⁽♭5⁾

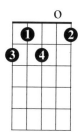

F#⁷⁽♭5⁾ ↔ G♭⁷⁽♭5⁾

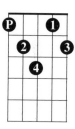

G⁷⁽♭5⁾

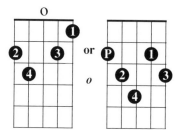

G#⁷⁽♭5⁾ ↔ A♭⁷⁽♭5⁾

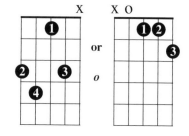

A⁷⁽♭5⁾

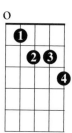

A#⁷⁽♭5⁾ ↔ B♭⁷⁽♭5⁾

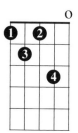

B⁷⁽♭5⁾

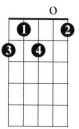

Dominant chords: Dominant seventh
with flatted ninth

*Acordes de dominante: Séptima de
dominante con novena bemol*

7(♭9)
seven flat nine
siete con novena bemol

C^{7(♭9)}

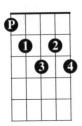

C^{♯7(♭9)} ↔ D^{♭7(♭9)}

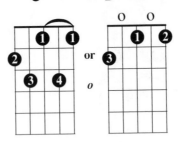

D^{7(♭9)}

D^{♯7(♭9)} ↔ E^{♭7(♭9)}

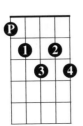

E^{7(♭9)}

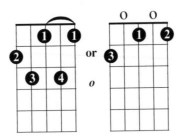

F^{7(♭9)}

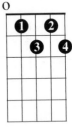

F^{♯7(♭9)} ↔ G^{♭7(♭9)}

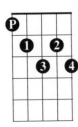

G^{7(♭9)}

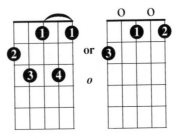

G^{♯7(♭9)} ↔ A^{♭7(♭9)}

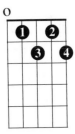

A^{7(♭9)}

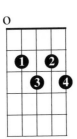

A^{♯7(♭9)} ↔ B^{♭7(♭9)}

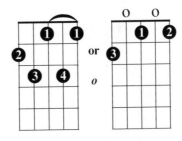

B^{7(♭9)}

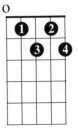

7(♯9)
seven sharp nine
siete con novena aumentada

C⁷⁽♯⁹⁾

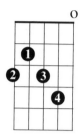

C♯⁷⁽♯⁹⁾ ↔ D♭⁷⁽♯⁹⁾

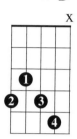

D⁷⁽♯⁹⁾

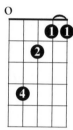

D♯⁷⁽♯⁹⁾ ↔ E♭⁷⁽♯⁹⁾

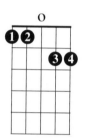

E⁷⁽♯⁹⁾

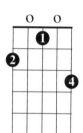

F⁷⁽♯⁹⁾

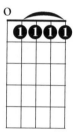

F♯⁷⁽♯⁹⁾ ↔ G♭⁷⁽♯⁹⁾

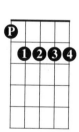

G⁷⁽♯⁹⁾

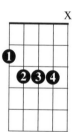

G♯⁷⁽♯⁹⁾ ↔ A♭⁷⁽♯⁹⁾

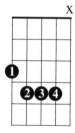

A⁷⁽♯⁹⁾

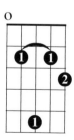

A♯⁷⁽♯⁹⁾ ↔ B♭⁷⁽♯⁹⁾

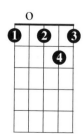

B⁷⁽♯⁹⁾

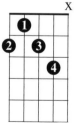

9
nine
nueve

C⁹

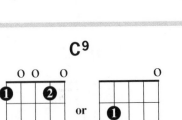

or

C♯⁹ ↔ D♭⁹

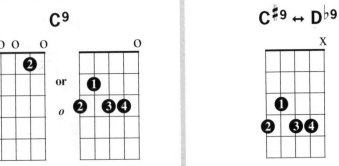

D⁹

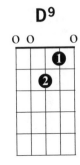

D♯⁹ ↔ E♭⁹

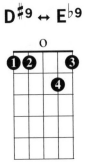

E⁹

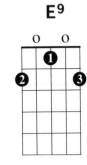

F⁹

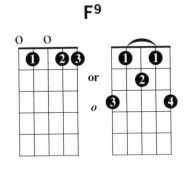

or

F♯⁹ ↔ G♭⁹

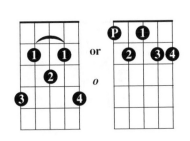

or

G⁹

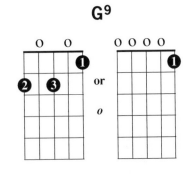

or

G♯⁹ ↔ A♭⁹

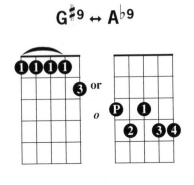

or

A⁹

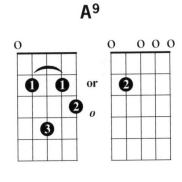

or

A♯⁹ ↔ B♭⁹

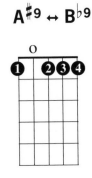

B⁹

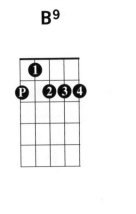

9(♭5)
nine flat five
nueve con quinta bemol

C$^{9(♭5)}$

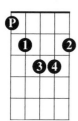

C$^{♯9(♭5)}$ ↔ D$^{♭9(♭5)}$

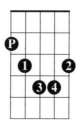

D$^{9(♭5)}$

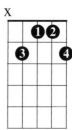

D$^{♯9(♭5)}$ ↔ E$^{♭9(♭5)}$

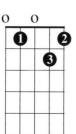

E$^{9(♭5)}$

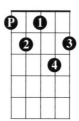

F$^{9(♭5)}$

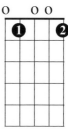

F$^{♯9(♭5)}$ ↔ G$^{♭9(♭5)}$

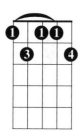

G$^{9(♭5)}$

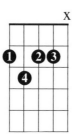

G$^{♯9(♭5)}$ ↔ A$^{♭9(♭5)}$

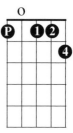

A$^{9(♭5)}$

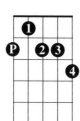

A$^{♯9(♭5)}$ ↔ B$^{♭9(♭5)}$

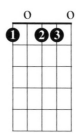

B$^{9(♭5)}$

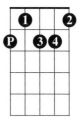

9(♯11)
nine sharp eleven
nueve con oncena aumentada

C⁹(♯11)

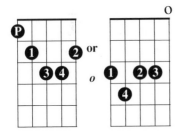

C♯9(♯11) ↔ D♭9(♯11)

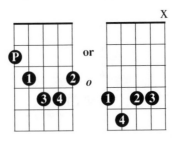

D⁹(♯11)

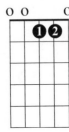

D♯9(♯11) ↔ E♭9(♯11)

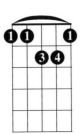

E⁹(♯11)

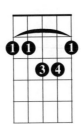

F⁹(♯11)

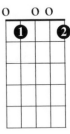

F♯9(♯11) ↔ G♭9(♯11)

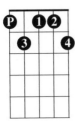

G⁹(♯11)

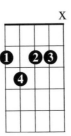

G♯9(♯11) ↔ A♭9(♯11)

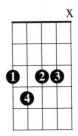

A⁹(♯11)

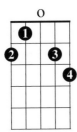

A♯9(♯11) ↔ B♭9(♯11)

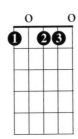

B⁹(♯11)

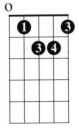

11
eleven
once

C¹¹

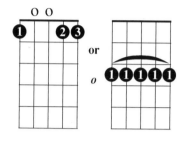

C♯¹¹ ↔ D♭¹¹

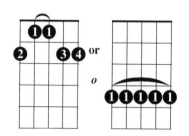

D¹¹

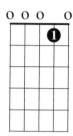

D♯¹¹ ↔ E♭¹¹

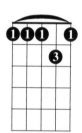

E¹¹

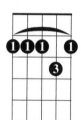

F¹¹

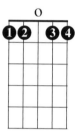

F♯¹¹ ↔ G♭¹¹

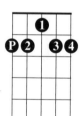

G¹¹

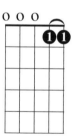

G♯¹¹ ↔ A♭¹¹

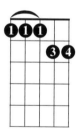

A¹¹

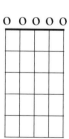

A♯¹¹ ↔ B♭¹¹

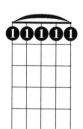

B¹¹

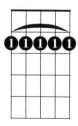

13
thirteen
trece

C^{13}

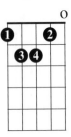

C$^{\sharp 13}$ ↔ D$^{\flat 13}$

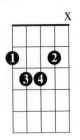

D^{13}

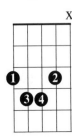

D$^{\sharp 13}$ ↔ E$^{\flat 13}$

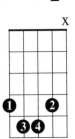

E^{13}

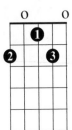

F^{13}

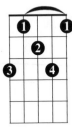

F$^{\sharp 13}$ ↔ G$^{\flat 13}$

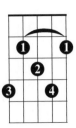

G^{13}

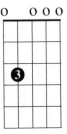

G$^{\sharp 13}$ ↔ A$^{\flat 13}$

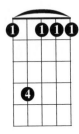

A^{13}

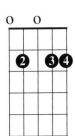

A$^{\sharp 13}$ ↔ B$^{\flat 13}$

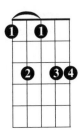

B^{13}

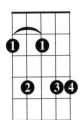

13(♭9)
tthirteen flat nine
trece con novena bemol

C^13(♭9)

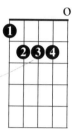

C^#13(♭9) ↔ D^♭13(♭9)

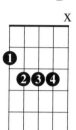

D^13(♭9)

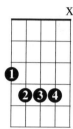

D^#13(♭9) ↔ E^♭13(♭9)

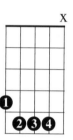

E^13(♭9)

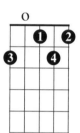

F^13(♭9)

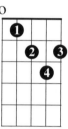

F^#13(♭9) ↔ G^♭13(♭9)

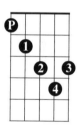

G^13(♭9)

G^#13(♭9) ↔ A^♭13(♭9)

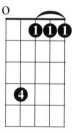

A^13(♭9)

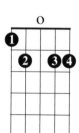

A^#13(♭9) ↔ B^♭13(♭9)

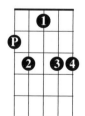

B^13(♭9)

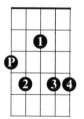

13($^{♭9}_{♭5}$)
thirteen flat nine, flat five
trece con novena bemol y quinta bemol

C$^{13(^{♭9}_{♭5})}$

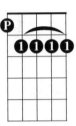

C$^{♯13(^{♭9}_{♭5})}$ ↔ D$^{♭13(^{♭9}_{♭5})}$

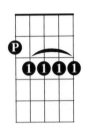

D$^{13(^{♭9}_{♭5})}$

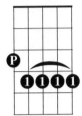

D$^{♯13(^{♭9}_{♭5})}$ ↔ E$^{♭13(^{♭9}_{♭5})}$

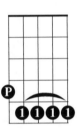

E$^{13(^{♭9}_{♭5})}$

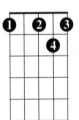

E$^{13(^{♭9}_{♭5})}$

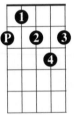

F$^{♯13(^{♭9}_{♭5})}$ ↔ G$^{♭13(^{♭9}_{♭5})}$

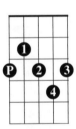

G$^{13(^{♭9}_{♭5})}$

G$^{♯13(^{♭9}_{♭5})}$ ↔ A$^{♭13(^{♭9}_{♭5})}$

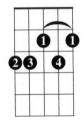

A$^{13(^{♭9}_{♭5})}$

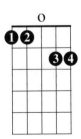

A$^{♯13(^{♭9}_{♭5})}$ ↔ B$^{♭13(^{♭9}_{♭5})}$

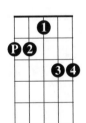

B$^{13(^{♭9}_{♭5})}$

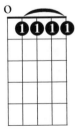

diminished
disminuido

C°

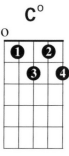

C#° ↔ D♭°

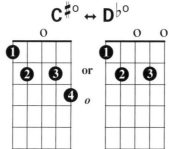

D°

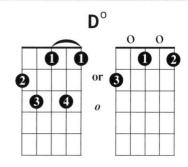

D#° ↔ E♭°

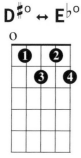

E°

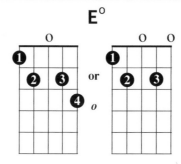

F°

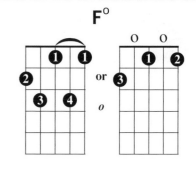

F#° ↔ G♭°

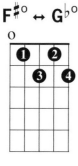

G°

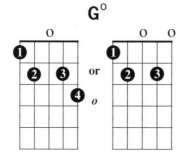

G#° ↔ A♭°

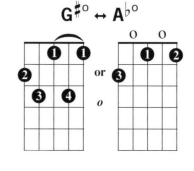

A°

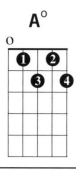

A#° ↔ B♭°

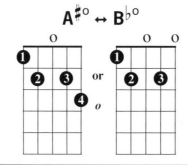

B°

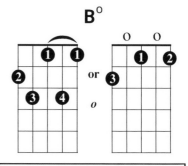

Note: In chord symbol notation for instruments of the guitar family, a "diminished chord" is assumed to be a diminished seventh chord, since the diminished triad is not commonly used with these instruments. There are basically only three diminished chord positions, each of which has four enharmonic equivalents.

Nota: En el cifrado para instrumentos de la familia de la guitarra, cuando se habla de un "acorde disminuido" se supone que se trata de un acorde de séptima disminuido, ya que poco se usa la triada disminuida con estos instrumentos. Básicamente hay tres posiciones de acorde disminuido, con cuatro equivalencias enarmónicas para cada una.

+
augmented
aumentado

C+
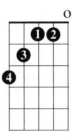

C♯+ ↔ D♭+
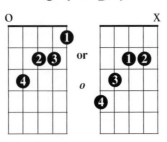

D+
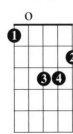

D♯+ ↔ E♭+
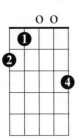

E+
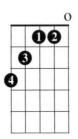

F+

F♯+ ↔ G♭+
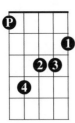

G+
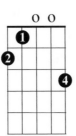

G♯+ ↔ A♭+
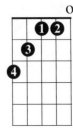

A+
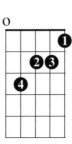

A♯+ ↔ B♭+
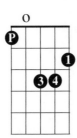

B+
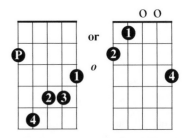

Observe the enharmonic equivalency between the chords on this page. There are basically only four augmented triad positions, each of which has three enharmonic equivalents.

Observe la equivalencia enarmónica entre los acordes de esta página. Básicamente existen sólo cuatro posiciones de triada aumentada, cada una de las cuales tiene tres equivalencias enarmónicas.

+7
augmented seven
siete con quinta aumentada

C+⁷

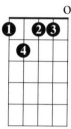

C#+⁷ ↔ D♭+⁷

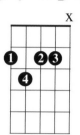

D+⁷

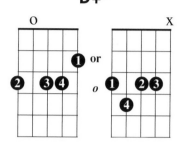

D#+⁷ ↔ E♭+⁷

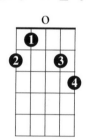

E+⁷

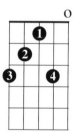

F+⁷

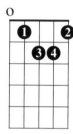

F#+⁷ ↔ G♭+⁷

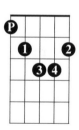

G+⁷

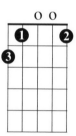

G#+⁷ ↔ A♭+⁷

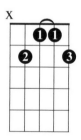

A+⁷

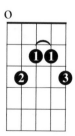

A#+⁷ ↔ B♭+⁷

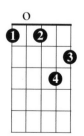

B+⁷

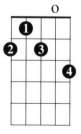

+⁷⁽♭⁹⁾
augmented seven flat nine
siete con quinta aumentada y novena bemol

C⁷⁺⁽♭⁹⁾
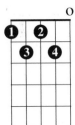

C♯⁷⁺⁽♭⁹⁾ ↔ D♭⁷⁺⁽♭⁹⁾
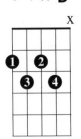

D⁷⁺⁽♭⁹⁾
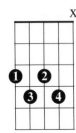

D♯⁷⁺⁽♭⁹⁾ ↔ E♭⁷⁺⁽♭⁹⁾
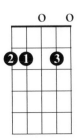

E⁷⁺⁽♭⁹⁾
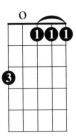

F⁷⁺⁽♭⁹⁾
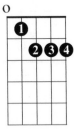

F♯⁷⁺⁽♭⁹⁾ ↔ G♭⁷⁺⁽♭⁹⁾
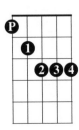

G⁷⁺⁽♭⁹⁾
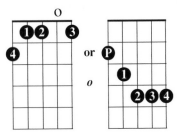

G♯⁷⁺⁽♭⁹⁾ ↔ A♭⁷⁺⁽♭⁹⁾
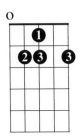

A⁷⁺⁽♭⁹⁾
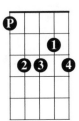

A♯⁷⁺⁽♭⁹⁾ ↔ B♭⁷⁺⁽♭⁹⁾
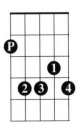

B⁷⁺⁽♭⁹⁾
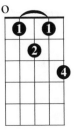

+9
augmented nine
nueve con quinta aumentada

C+9
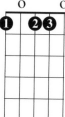

C#+9 ↔ Db+9
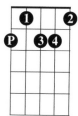

D+9
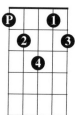

D#+9 ↔ Eb+9
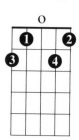

E+9
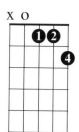

F+9

F#+9 ↔ Gb+9
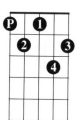

G+9
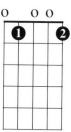

G#+9 ↔ Ab+9
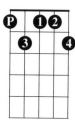

A+9
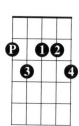

A#+9 ↔ Bb+9
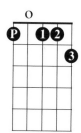

B+9
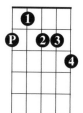

sus
suspended
sus

C sus

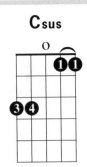

C#sus ↔ D♭sus

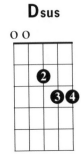

D sus

D#sus ↔ E♭sus

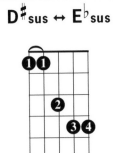

E sus

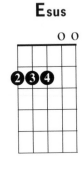

F sus

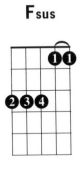

F#sus ↔ G♭sus

G sus

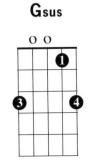

G#sus ↔ A♭sus

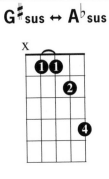

A sus

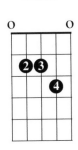

A#sus ↔ B♭sus

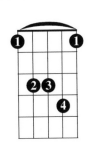

B sus

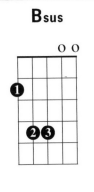

⁷sus
seven suspended
siete sus

C⁷sus
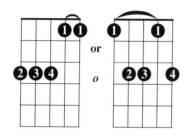

C^{#7}sus ↔ D^{♭7}sus
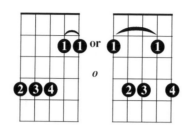

D⁷sus

D^{#7}sus4 ↔ E^{♭7}sus
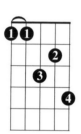

E⁷sus
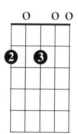

F⁷sus
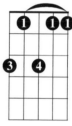

F^{#7}sus ↔ G^{♭7}sus
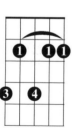

G⁷sus
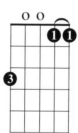

G^{#7}sus ↔ A^{♭7}sus
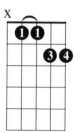

A⁷sus
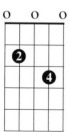

A^{#7}sus ↔ B^{♭7}sus
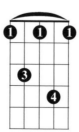

B⁷sus
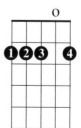

About the author

José Guadalupe Alfaro is one of the most sought after vihuela players in the mariachi world. Born in Mexico City in 1959, he began his musical career in the mid-1970's, in the famous Plaza Garibaldi. He studied music formally at the Escuela Libre de Música, the Mexico City musician's union (SUTM) school, and with private teachers. Through the seventies and eighties, Alfaro worked in many hotels, restaurants, and nightclubs of Mexico's capital city, where — as a member of Mariachi México '70, Mariachi Oro y Plata, Mariachi Dos Mil, Los Monarcas and other groups — he accompanied such artists as Lucha Villa, María de Lourdes, Felipe Arriaga, Gerardo Reyes, Beatriz Adriana, Gilberto Valenzuela, Pandora, and Joan Sebastián. In 1988, he joined Mariachi Águilas de América, the mariachi that recorded most prolifically during the 1990s, and with which he remained for over a decade. Alfaro has recorded extensively with artists such as Pepe Aguilar, José Guadalupe Esparza, Alejandro Fernández, Pedro Fernández, Vicente Fernández, Rocío Dúrcal, Hermanas Huerta, Lucero, Lupita D'Alessio, Ángeles Ochoa, Paquita la del Barrio, Julio Preciado, Marco Antonio Solís, Juan Valentín, and Alicia Villarreal. In addition to being a current member of Mariachi México de Pepe Villa, he is musical director and arranger for several singers, including Guadalupe Pineda, Ángeles Ochoa, and Alberto Vázquez. Despite his busy schedule of recordings, performances, and tours, Alfaro still finds time to teach private students.

Sobre el autor

José Guadalupe Alfaro es uno de los vihuelistas más solicitados en el mundo del mariachi. Nacido en la Ciudad de México en 1959, comenzó su carrera como músico en la famosa Plaza Garibaldi, a mediados de los años setenta. Cursó estudios formales en la Escuela Libre de Música, la escuela del Sindicato Único de Trabajadores de la Música (SUTM) y con maestros particulares. Durante los años setenta y ochenta —como integrante del Mariachi México '70, Mariachi Oro y Plata, Mariachi 2000, Los Monarcas y otras agrupaciones— trabajó en diferentes restaurantes, hoteles y centros nocturnos de la ciudad capital, donde acompañaba a artistas como Lucha Villa, María de Lourdes, Felipe Arriaga, Gerardo Reyes, Beatriz Adriana, Gilberto Valenzuela, Pandora y Joan Sebastián. En 1988 ingresó al Mariachi Águilas de América, el mariachi que mayor número de grabaciones realizó durante los años noventa, con el cual permaneció por más de una década. Ha grabado extensivamente con artistas como Pepe Aguilar, José Guadalupe Esparza, Alejandro Fernández, Pedro Fernández, Vicente Fernández, Rocío Dúrcal, Hermanas Huerta, Lucero, Lupita D'Alessio, Ángeles Ochoa, Paquita la del Barrio, Julio Preciado, Marco Antonio Solís, Juan Valentín y Alicia Villarreal, entre otros. Además de ser integrante actual del Mariachi México de Pepe Villa, trabaja como director musical y arreglista para varios cantantes, incluyendo a Ángeles Ochoa, Guadalupe Pineda y Alberto Vázquez. Entre su apretado itinerario de grabaciones, actuaciones y giras, aun encuentra tiempo para impartir sus conocimientos a alumnos particulares.

Made in the USA
Coppell, TX
14 April 2024

31278432R00024